*To Jill
With best wishes from Ge...*

PREFAC

We are most grateful to South East Arts, and in parti... helping this book to see the light of day by means of a grant, and for judith's general encouragement of folk-related activities and of our research, events and teaching in this area.

We have focused on the three counties covered by South East Arts, but Surrey fanatics will, however, notice a considerable Kent and Sussex bias in this book, which is partly due to our lesser knowledge of Surrey, but partly to the sad fact that less traditional culture survives or is on record in that county.

The book concentrates on three rituals, two of which are common to all three counties and one only found in Kent. We have tried to provide as many source accounts as possible, so that the reader has the facts on which to base his own conclusions. We have also included various ideas as to origins and significance and some of our own interpretations. But we have tried throughout the text to separate fact from speculation.

Very little has been written about apple wassailing in the south-east, particularly on the deeds of the legendary Duncton wassailers, and we are delighted to have the opportunity to remedy this gap. Rosemary Gilmour, Assistant Curator of Chichester District Museum (of whom more in the acknowledgements) has been particularly helpful on the Duncton tradition and on West Sussex Tipteering.

There is quite a lot of knowledge and accounts of Mummers Plays scattered round the three counties, but we feel there is a need to gather this together for the use of future researchers. We have been teaching Mummers Plays both as part of academic disciplines and as practical workshop ritual drama in the area for many years as well as running The Tonbridge Mummers & Hoodeners, and are well placed with documents and contacts to provide such a focus.

As Percy Maylam's marvellous book on 'The Hooden Horse' is as rare as the creature (limited edition), we have taken this opportunity to quote substantial parts of the sightings of this remarkable beast (as opposed to the analogies and theories) recorded in his book (both his own first hand accounts and those from newspapers etc he has gleaned from the past). To this we have added information from elsewhere and documented the revival of the custom.

We should be extremely grateful if readers could point out any errors of fact or interpretation in our text and send us any further information they may have on these three fascinating customs.

Geoff and Fran Doel
Tonbridge
1992

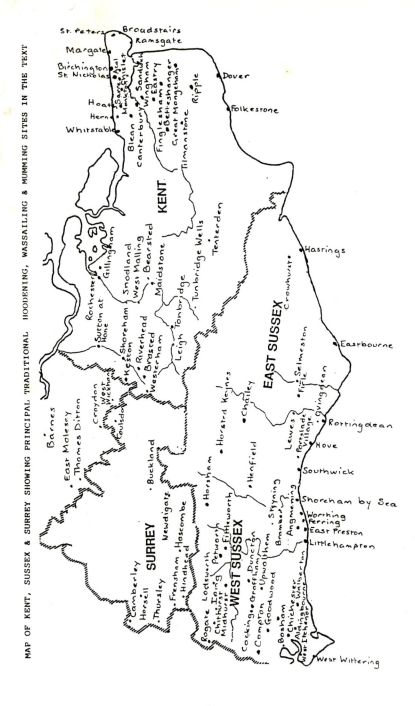

MAP OF KENT, SUSSEX & SURREY SHOWING PRINCIPAL TRADITIONAL HOODENING, WASSAILING & MUMMING SITES IN THE 'TEXT'

THE MIDWINTER FESTIVAL IN THE SOUTH-EAST

The customs considered in this book are rituals performed in the Midwinter period (from mid-December to mid-January) and which therefore have relevance to the Twelve Days of Christmas, the Midwinter Solstice or New Year. We would define a ritual as a regular seasonal ceremony with set locations, actions, costumes, music and speech.

The book's area in the counties of Kent, Sussex and Surrey is largely determined by its association with South-East Arts, but these counties (particularly Kent and Sussex) share much in common as well as mutual boundaries. All three have the mixture of chalk and sandstone hills and clay lowlands which make for varied agriculture; they have all had extensive areas of orchards in the past and farm and itinerant workers regularly passed from one to the other, helping to spread songs and customs. All three have had to cope with proximity to London and interaction with the culture of the upper and middle classes, through landowners and clergy whose more sophisticated tastes followed the fashions of London and the intellectual lead of Oxford, Cambridge and Canterbury. London has always been an important market for the agricultural produce of the counties and many of those involved in traditional customs had links with London. For the past 100 years the three counties have provided homes for thousands of daily commuters into the Capital. The toll on Surrey traditional culture has been high, but Kent and Sussex have retained much of their lore and many of their customs have survived or been revived.

Kent, Sussex and Surrey were heavily settled by the Anglo-Saxons from the fifth century AD and many aspects of their Christmas celebrations are absorbed from pagan Midwinter yule celebrations when they feasted and drank to each other's health using the term 'wassail!' — 'Be of good health!' (traditionally said to have been introduced into Kent by Hengist and his daughter Rowena). The Germanic Midwinter period was marked by mistletoe, the yule log or ashen faggot, the evergreen holly and ivy and ceremonies of Blessing the Plough. Even the door-to-door visitations of carol singers with their Christian carols relate to the earlier wassailers with their wassail bowl and Midwinter songs about food, drink and good luck.

Germanic paganism, seen in the names of the days of the week which commemorate their gods Tyr, Woden, Thor and Frigg, is also detectable in the Mummers Plays, gift-bearing and feasting at the Midwinter Solstice and New Year and the Horse Cult, though some elements may derive from (or be shared by) earlier Celtic culture. Indeed one of the greatest mistakes among 'earth mysteries' writers today is the assumption that there was only one pagan culture preceding the Christian; the situation is much more complex.

The Tonbridge Mummers & Hoodeners and Alan Austen Blessing the Plough at the Kent Museum of Rural Life, New Year's Day 1992. (Photo: Simon Evans)

Despite the fact that nineteenth century folklorists overestimated the influence of Roman culture on our folk customs, we should remember that the Christian conversion in the south-east was by those steeped in a Roman culture which had absorbed aspects of pre-Christian Roman practices, particularly as regards Midwinter festivities. Our 'Twelve Days of Christmas' have a rather shadowy origin, but they do probably derive from the tripartite Roman Midwinter celebrations of Saturnalia (a lighthearted 'fun' festival in honour of the ancient god of agriculture), a one-day serious religious festival commemorating Sol Invictus (The Unconquered Sun) held on 25th December (later identified specifically with the Emperor), and, finally, Kalends, a jolly welcoming in of the New Year. The date of Christ's birth being unknown the Church selected 25th December as Christ's birthdate to take over the associations and iconography of these earlier Roman, Eastern and Germanic festivals.

It seems to be, too, from the Roman festival of the Saturnalia that the medieval concept of the Lord of Misrule stems. The 'Lord' presided over bizarre activities over the Twelve Days of Christmas in which order was inverted. In pagan Rome, slaves were sometimes served by their masters during the Saturnalia; a variant of this practice, officers serving men, survived in some of the armed forces until recently. The following account discovered in the records of the Chichester Consistory Court concerns allegations of misconduct in a clergyman and refers to a Lord of Misrule in 1586/7:

'Mr H. Weston 4th day of March 1586/7 appeared and objected to the charge that he played at tables all night in an Inn in the city of Chichester publicly to the slander of his function. He alleged that he was sent for by virtue of a Commission from my Lord Admiral to be examined about certain marine causes the 30th day of December last and being in the town somewhat late so that he could not be dispatched to return home again the same night, he went to the sign of the Swan for lodging where being on the next day in the morning about eight of the clock he played at the tables with the goodman of the house and he had not played above an hour's space but that one William Brunne who then played the part of a lord of misrule came in where this examinate was at play and said that that game was an Christmas game and so perforce took this examinate from thence and made him ride over a staff to the Cross.'

In church ritual a similar effect was achieved at Midwinter with the tradition of the Boy Bishop, where in some cathedrals a choirboy was elected as a mock bishop for a short period over part of the Christmas celebrations. The child vested in costly robes identical to those of a bishop, was led in procession through the streets at Christmastime, and is believed to have addressed the cathedral congregation from the pulpit. There are records of a Boy Bishop custom at Salisbury, Rochester and Canterbury and the Chichester Cathedral accounts for 1534/35 have *'Item for new makyng the robe of scarlet for the chyld boysshop to Lawrence 10d'*. Unfortunately, Salisbury Cathedral no longer supports the suggestion put forward in many books on folklore that the tiny 'bishop's tomb' in its nave is for a Boy Bishop who died in office and was buried with full rites in the Cathedral. 'Blessing the Plough' was Christianised in many areas and the Young Farmers usually bless a plough at Chichester Cathedral in December.

Early missionaries in the south of England such as Augustine in Kent were advised to retain as many aspects of paganism as were compatible with the new faith so as not to alienate their new flock. Wells dedicated to pagan deities were re-dedicated to Christian saints, pagan sites were re-used as Christian churches and some seasonal rituals and festivals were absorbed into the Christian calendar. The church remained uneasy about stone worship and well worship, which are mentioned as punishable offences in many Anglo-Saxon codes of laws, but most offensive were animal disguise customs which were held to be particularly obnoxious to the Christian faith. Animal disguise customs were prevalent in pagan Rome and the earlier Augustine, Bishop of Hippo, was sufficiently concerned about them in the fourth century to write:

'If you ever hear of anyone carrying out that most filfthy practice of dressing up like a horse or a stag, chastise him most severely.'

THE KENTISH HOODEN HORSE

Midwinter rituals in which men disguise themselves as horses and horned animals are widespread in Britain and many other parts of Europe. The church, although anxious to absorb as many aspects of paganism as were compatible with Christianity, was decidedly uneasy about anything to do with animal worship. As recently as the 1950s, Bert Lloyd was told of a case in the Balkans where a young man was warned by his priest that if he died whilst dressed up as a horse his soul would be forfeit.

In Britain we find remnants of Midwinter horse disguise customs in Ireland, South Wales, Dorset, Lancashire, Cheshire, Northamptonshire, the borders of Yorkshire, Derbyshire and Nottinghamshire and in East Kent. Horse skulls seem to have had ritual significance as far back as stone age and bronze age cultures, judging from their use and alignment in burials. The horse cult was particularly strong amongst the Celtic peoples as evinced by the carving of the Uffington White Horse and the story of Rhiannon in *Pwyll, Prince of Dyfed* in *The Mabinogion*. The Romano-Gallic peoples worshipped a horse goddess, Epona, and a number of statues and altars from her cult survive in Britain and Europe.

Tacitus in the first century AD records that the Germans on the continent kept white horses which were thought to be 'privy to the gods' counsels' and which were therefore used for the purpose of divination. The Vikings are recorded as using horses' skulls on poles to work magic. The souling plays at Antrobus and other Cheshire villages, which feature a horse's skull on a pole held by a man covered in sacking, could derive from Celtic or Scandinavian culture. The horses' heads used in these plays were regarded as good luck talismans and were often buried in the villages between the yearly performances. To steal the horses' head from another village would be to double the good fortune of one's own village during the coming year.

No Midwinter horse customs survive in Sussex and Surrey but there is a Hooden Horse tradition in Kent which relates to the Isle of Thanet and to Walmer and Deal. Thanet was the earliest Anglo-Saxon settlement in Kent and according to early chronicles was given by the British King Vortigern to his Saxon Federati led by Hengist and Horsa (whose names mean 'stallion' and 'mare' and may therefore be indicative of a Horse Cult). Horse disguise rituals survive in Germanic folk customs.

Hoodeners — details unknown? — East Kent 1940s. Authors would appreciate any further information on this picture. (Photo: Doc Roe Collection)

Unlike the Souling Horse of Cheshire and the Mari Lwyd ('The Pale Mare') of South Wales, the Kent Hooden Horse generally had a carved wooden head, though several nineteenth century sources talk of a dead horse's head being used (these references all seem to derive from one source). As with other horse disguise customs, a man covered in cloth or sacking took the part of the horse, stooping to make a back, clasping the pole attached to the head and opening and closing the horse's jaws by means of a string. A 'Waggoner' was in charge of the horse and a 'Jockey' attempted to ride him (these two roles were sometimes combined in other customs). There were attendant musicians and, in common with the Mari Lwyd custom, a man disguised as a woman with blackened face and besom broom (the 'Mollie'), often attended the horse as well. The sweeper figure is frequently found at solstical celebrations. In Shakespeare's *A Midsummer Night's Dream*, Puck sweeps with his broom at the end of the play while the marriages are being consummated at the solstice as part of a ritual to bless the progeny of the unions and to ensure they are born free from deformity:

> 'not a mouse
> Shall disturb this hallowed house.
> I am sent with broom before,
> To sweep the dust behind the door'...
>
> 'Never mole, hare-lip, nor scar,
> Nor mark prodigious, such as are
> Despised in nativity,
> Shall upon their children be.'

In Yorkshire groups of guisers used to sweep through houses unannounced with besom brooms at New Year and the sweeper is a common figure in the Mummers Play. The man–woman figure appears in many Midwinter and Summer customs and is presumably emblematic of fertility.

The name 'Hooden' may relate to the hooded appearance of the horse, although some writers have suggested a connection with 'wooden', the Anglo-Saxon god Woden and even Robin Hood! The pronunciation of the 'oo' sound in the Thanet dialect was close to the Germanic 'u' with umlaut and the 'h' was dropped, giving a pronunciation of 'uden'. As Dr Cawte points out in his *Ritual Animal Disguise*, were it named after the Germanic god Woden, one would expect the 'w' sound to have been retained in the East Kent dialect as in the Kent place name Woodnesborough near Ash (thought to be named after Woden) or the day of the week 'Wednesday' which certainly was named after the god.

However, the Scandinavian equivalent of Woden, Odinn, appears at the Midwinter season as a visiting gift-bringer and has links with Scandinavian Midwinter folk customs (ie The Sword Dance) which were introduced into other parts of Britain. So a link between the Hooden Horse and the cult of Woden is possible and the custom is almost certainly descended from either a Germanic or Celtic pagan Midwinter ritual. There is an interesting reference to Midwinter animal disguise customs in the *Penitential* of Archbishop Theodore (died 690) who decreed penances for three years for 'any who on the kalends of January clothe themselves with the skins of cattle and carry heads of animals'. He condemns this practice as being 'daemoniacum'.

Robin Hood is probably too late a folklore figure to be connected with the origins of the Hooden Horse and in any case is usually connected with the May Games rather than Midwinter customs.

A Canterbury solicitor, Percy Maylam, wrote the definitive book on the Hooden Horse in a limited edition in 1909. Maylam realised that the tradition was in danger of becoming extinct and decided to trace its earlier documentary history and to research the last surviving remnants of it in his own day. His work recounts book and newspaper references to the custom in the eighteenth and nineteenth centuries and describes his own sightings of the Horse at Monkton, St Nicholas at Wade, Walmer and Deal.

Maylam first saw the Hooden Horse while spending Christmases with his uncle at Gore Street, Monkton, from 1888-1892:

'Anyone who has spent a Christmas in a farm-house in Thanet — it has been my good fortune to spend five — will not forget Christmas Eve; when seated round the fire, one hears the banging of gates and tramping of feet on the gravel paths outside (or, if the weather be seasonable, the more cheerful crunching of crisp snow), and the sound of loud clapping. Everybody springs up saying: "The hooodeners have come, let us go and see the fun." The front door is flung open, and there they all are outside, the 'Waggoner' cracking his whip and leading the Horse (the man who plays this part is called the "Hoodener"), which assumes a most restive manner, champing his teeth, and rearing and plunging, and doing his best to unseat the "Rider", who tries to mount him, while the "Waggoner" shouts "whoa!" and snatches at the bridle. "Mollie" is there also! She is a lad dressed up in woman's clothes and vigorously sweeps the ground behind the horse with a birch broom. There are generally two or three other performers besides, who play the concertina, tambourine or instruments of that kind. The performance goes on for some time, and such of the spectators as wish to do so, try to mount and ride the horse, but with poor success. All sorts of antics take place, Mollie has been known to stand on her head, exhibiting nothing more alarming in the way of lingerie than a pair of hobnail boots with the appropriate setting of corduroy trousers. Beer and largesse are dispensed and the performers go further. Singing of songs and carols is not usually a part of the performance and no set words are spoken. In Thanet, occasionally, but not always, the performers, or some of them, blacken their faces. Years ago, smock frocks were the regulation dress of the party.

'In a house which possesses a large hall, the performers are often invited inside; at times the horse uses little ceremony, and opening the door, walks in uninvited... Without doubt the Hoodeners are seen at their best outdoors — and in the court or on the lawn of some old farm-house, for then the eyes of the spectators coming fresh from the light inside take only an impressionistic

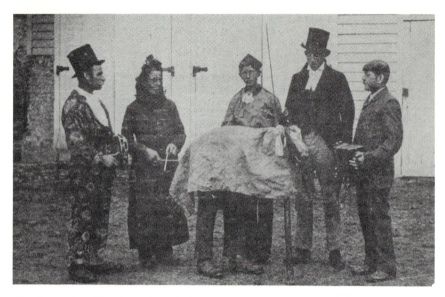
Hoodeners from Hale Farm, St Nicholas at Wade, photographed by Percy Maylam in 1905.

Hoodeners at St Nicholas-at-Wade c1908.
(Photo by permission of University of Newcastle upon Tyne)

picture of the scene, and the horse in the dim winter's night, made even more indistinct by occasional cross rays of flickering light from the windows, becomes a monster of weird and awesome possibilities.'

'Good old hooden horse — the possible frightener of children and to those no longer children the bringer-back of memories of happy frights when once they were. "Is this the hooden horse coming round?" is the first enquiry of the exile on his return home for Christmas after years of absence.'

In 1905 Percy Maylam arranged to photograph a team of Hoodeners from Hale Farm, St Nicholas at Wade (between Margate and Canterbury). The men in the team were employed with the horses on the farm and Maylam explains that this was traditionally the case since it was the custom to bleed Kent farm horses just before Christmas and then let them rest before ploughing which began after Plough Monday. Thus the men in charge of the horses had little to do workwise for the period over Christmas and took out a mock horse instead. The photographic session was arranged out of season at Bolingbroke Farm, Sarre and the Mollie (whose role had recently lapsed) was specially revived (the Hoodeners seen by Maylam at Gore Street, 1888-92, had a Mollie). No besom broom was immediately to hand and Maylam's first photograph shows Mollie playing the triangle, while somebody was busy at work behind the scenes making the besom shown in his second photo. This is how Maylam describes the St Nicholas horse:

'The ears are pointed pieces of leather. The head is decorated with all the trappings usual in the case of a Kent farm horse in that district when dressed in state. On the top of the head, between the ears, with a swinging disc, is the head brass, and on the forehead the circular brass ornament called the face piece... the tail is made of a small piece of horsehair decorated with caytis. The bridle is a long piece of leather thickly covered with brass studs.'

Maylam interviewed men who had personal knowledge of the custom at St Nicholas extending back at least to the eighteen forties. His interest in the St Nicholas Horse came as a stimulus, when in common with other hoodening traditions, it was on the wane. A photograph survives of the team in 1908 with a revival of Mollie as a permanent fixture. Although the custom lapsed for a time, the village never forgot it and it was revived in 1966. Researcher Simon Evans has tape recorded the reminiscences of the 'rider' in the photo, Tom West, who lived at St Nicholas all his life.

Maylam next decided to photograph and interview a team of hoodeners in action:

'On Christmas Eve 1906, I went to Walmer, and having ascertained the time when the party would set out, I had a comfortable tea at the hotel near Walmer Station. While at tea, a man in grotesque attire came into the room, and proceeded to blacken his face with burnt cork at the fire. I, who had thoughts for nothing but hoodening, enquired if he were one of that party. "No," he said, and it appeared he was one of the Walmer minstrels with no very great opinion of such obsolescent customs as hoodening.

Hoodeners at Walmer; described by Maylam, Christmas Eve 1906; photographed by him March 1907.

'However, very shortly afterwards, the well-known clap! clap! was heard from within the bar — the Hoodeners had come. I hastened to see them. The party consisted of four: the hoodener with the horse's head, the man whose duty it is to lead the horse, and when not doing so, to play the triangle, and two musicians, one playing the tambourine and the other the concertina.'

'... Here I found the practice was that the "gratuity" had to be placed in the horse's jaws, and...the horse put his head on the counter of the bar while the landlord's little daughter was lifted up from the other side in order to carry out the proper form of giving the money, after conquering her fright, real or feigned.'

'...Mr Robert Laming told me...that he had been out with his horse on Christmas Eve for this five and twenty years and missed doing so only one year. The Walmer party were in their ordinary clothes, but formerly I was told, they wore smock frocks; they had no Mollie, nor any recollection of her. I accompanied the party a little way on their rounds which I was told would not finish till about eleven o'clock: it was then six-thirty, and I found the Hoodeners sure of their welcome, the horse gambolled into all the crowded shops, and at Christmas they are crowded, and every one was pleased except a collie dog which worked himself into a fearful rage but feared to try his teeth against the wooden jaws of the horse. On visiting the butcher, he, regardless of the graminivorous habits of the animal, placed a mutton chop in the jaws besides the accustomed tribute, a piece of humour which met with great applause.'

The St Nicholas-at-Wade Hoodener and Horse photographed by Percy Maylam in 1905.

The Walmer Hoodener and Horse photographed by Percy Maylam in 1907.

Robert Laming and his brother, William, and son, Joseph, played the music and Harry Axon carried the horse. Maylam did not photograph the Walmer Hoodeners until the following March.

In 1909 Percy Maylam documented the Deal Hoodeners, whom he found to be currently only two in number:

'Mr Robert Skardon told me that he has lived in Deal all the 53 years of his life and had always known the custom. When he was a lad his father used to have a hooden horse party: he carried the head, his father played the drum, his Uncle John Beaney the fiddle, and old Harry Chorner the piccolo. For many years there has been no "Mollie", but formerly the party included a man dressed up in woman's clothes, who was known as "Daisy". I could find no recollection of any beginning, Skardon's uncle Beaney, who died about two years ago, aged 75, had been at it all his life and his father before him. Skardon himself...about 20 years ago started a Christmas band and discontinued the horse, but notwithstanding, the hooden horse is not extinct. On Skardon discontinuing it, the custom was and is kept up by Mr Elbridge Bowles of Great Mongeham; he is one of Skardon's band, but after Christmas he and one other man go round with the horse, he plays the tin whistle while the other man represents the horse. They do Deal, but finding the country districts welcome them more, of late years they have visited

The Deal Hoodeners photographed by Percy Maylam in 1909.

Finglesham, Ripple, Tilmanstone, Eastry and Betteshanger. At the time of the South African War the horse was, with great success, got up with full military equipment.

'...The head (of the Deal horse) displays a marked variance from the others. It no doubt marks a comparatively modern departure from the usual archaic type, evidently showing an attempt to be more realistic. The forehead is covered with black plush in representation of a horse's coat, the ears are made of the same material and the eyes are painted in. The animal has departed from the agricultural type, in that, between the ears, a rosette is substituted in the place of the swinging brass disc of the Thanet horse or the three bells of the Walmer horse. The covering in this case is a dark green material, a kind of box-cloth, which at one time may very well have been the lining to a billiard table or bagatelle board.'

This account of the considerable changes to the make-up and venues of one Hooden Horse Party over 20 years is a warning to anyone assuming a static custom in the past, though one would expect greater changes to the custom at the end of the nineteenth century than earlier in the century.

Percy Maylam's description of the custom at Deal was seconded by a charming account sent to us in the early 1980s by Mrs Naomi Wiffen of

Edenbridge who saw the Deal horse as a small girl and whose account adds much fascinating detail:

'I remember as a child being taken out on Christmas Eve to the High Street in Deal where the shops would be open very late, and it was the only time Deal children were allowed out in the evening, as parents were very strict. As we would be looking at the lighted shops, and listening to the people selling their wares, a horrible growl, and a long horse's face would appear, resting on our shoulder and when one looked round, there would be a long row of teeth snapping at us with its wooden jaws. It was frightening for a child. Usually, there would be a man leading the horse, with a rope, and another covered over with sacks or blankets as the horse.'

The Deal Museum displays two accounts of the Hooden Horse at the turn of the century, one calling it the 'Green Horse' and mentioning that it was accompanied by handbell ringing. The other account is from an old lady who was a member of a Deal boatman's family and who calls it the 'Ogling Horse':

'Then there was the Ogling Horse — the hooded horse of Queen Elizabeth's reign, a man under a sack, with a wooden head something like a horse with two large clappers for a mouth, the man clapped them together with a terrible noise but that was part of Christmas.'

The earliest reference that Maylam traced to hoodening was in Dr Samuel Pegge's *Alphabet of Kenticisms:*

'Hooding (huo.ding) a country masquerade at Christmas time which in Derb, they call guising...and in other places mumming.'

A letter to the *European Magazine* in 1807 (much re-used by later nineteenth century folklorists) provides a reference to a dead horse's head being used and also mentions handbells and carols which (according to Maylam) were not a regular feature of the custom later (though mentioned in one of the Deal accounts quoted above):

'Also at Ramsgate, in Kent, I found they begin the festivities of Christmas by a curious procession: a party of young people procure the head of a dead horse, which is affixed to a pole about ten feet in length; a string is affixed to the lower jaw; a horse-cloth is also attached to the whole, under which one of the party gets, and by frequently pulling the string, keeps up a loud snapping noise, and is accompanied by the rest of the party, grotesquely habited, with handbells; they thus proceed from house to house, ringing their bells, and singing carols and songs; they are commonly gratified with beer and cake, or perhaps with money. This is called, provincially, a Hodening, and the figure above described a Hoden, or Woden horse.'

An addition to this account of 1825 extends the account to say:

'This curious ceremony is always observed in the Isle of Thanet on Christmas Eve; and is supposed to be an ancient relic of a festival, ordained to commemorate our Saxon ancestors' landing in that island.'

There are several references to Hooden Horses at Minster — eg in 1864, 'hooded horses not hooded quite up to the old style, perambulated the streets' *(Thanet Advertiser)* and in 1868:

'Hoodening was also the order of the evening on Christmas Eve...we fear carolling does not improve, and the jingling noise called hand-bell ringing was fearful. The hooden horse, we thought, was as extinct as the megatharium, but there was one that came again to see how the world was jogging on.' (Kent Herald)

Other references mention the custom at Broadstairs, St Peter's, St Lawrence, St Nicholas, Acol, Monkton and Birchington, calling at houses and the 'old woman' sweeping the feet of those who answered the door.

A very detailed account was sent to *The Church Times* in 1891 concerning the custom in the 1840s:

'When I was a lad, about 45 years since, it was always the custom on Christmas Eve with the male farm-servants from every farm in our parish of Hoath (Borough of Reculver) and neighbouring parishes of Herne and Chislet, to go round in the evening from house to house with the Hoodining Horse, which consisted of the imitation of a horse's head made of wood, life-size, fixed on a stick about the length of a broom handle; the lower jaw of the head was made to open with hinges, a hole was made through the roof of the mouth, then another through the forehead coming out by the throat, through this was passed a cord attached to the lower jaw, which when pulled by the cord at the throat caused it to close and open; on the lower jaw large-headed hob-nails were driven in to form the teeth. The strongest of the lads was selected for the horse; he stooped and made as long a back as he could, supporting himself with the stick carrying the head; then he was covered with a horse cloth, and one of his companions mounted his back. The horse had a bridle and reins. Then commenced the kicking, rearing, jumping, etc, etc, and the banging together of the teeth. As soon as the doors were opened the "horse" would pull his string incessantly, and the noise made can be better imagined than described. I confess that in my very young days I was horrified at the approach of the hoodining horse, but as I grew older I used to go round with them... There was no singing going on with the hoodining horse, and the party was strictly confined to the young men who went with the horses on the farms. I have seen some of the wooden heads carved out quite hollow in the throat part, and two holes bored through the forehead to form the eyes. The lad who played the horse would hold a lighted candle in the hollow, and you can imagine how horrible it was to one who opened the door to see such a thing close to his eyes. Carollers in those days were called hoodiners in the parishes I have named.'

A Mr Whitehead gave Percy Maylam a good account of the Birchington tradition on Christmas Eve in about 1855, when he remembers seeing at least three parties from the neighbouring farm-houses, where the farm hands lodged on the farm. One was the 'groom' and held the bridle, the second the 'horse', covered with a cloth, the third a slim youth who was the 'jockey', the fourth an 'old woman' who carried a broom and the fifth collected the 'oof' in a tinder box:

'The party first sang a country song, and knocked at the door. On opening the door the scene that presented itself was a prancing horse, opening and closing its jaws with a loud snapping noise, the groom shouting "whoa", the jockey attempting to mount, the old lady busy sweeping and the collector looking on. If invited into the kitchen, the acting would be continued there...'

Maidstone Museum has two Hooden Horses which were found in a barn at Wingham. These are most interesting, but are in poor condition. One is quite small (perhaps 3ft 6ins with wooden pole fixed) and could be for a child. The horse has leather ears, and nostrils are cut out and the eyes indented and is painted black, red and white, with a blanket covering and jaw that is pulled open and shut with a string, stones being fixed in the jaw to create the snapping noise.

The second head seems to be full sized, but lacks its pole and its string is broken. It also has stones for teeth and a horse brass on its forehead and a rosette. It has a studded belt and a mane of coloured streamers. There is also a Hooden Horse at Folkestone Library.

St Nicholas at Wade has two old Hooden Horses and one of them, in the possession of the Trice family for 130 years, is thought to be the one photographed by Maylam and is used in the revival started in 1966, which features a Waggoner, a Mate, Mollie, Farmer's Boy, Horse and Fiddler. One new feature is the writing of a topical village play each year. There has been a revival at Whitstable since the Second World War, where the horse is decorated with oyster shells. The Tonbridge Mummers and Hoodeners have been performing a West Kent Hooden Horse Play since 1981, although admittedly the tradition appears to lie solely in the eastern part of the county.

APPLE HOWLING OR WASSAILING

Apple wassailing, 'worsling' or 'howling' as it is called in different parts of the south and west, seems in origin to be a piece of sympathetic magic in which a libation of cider punch was given to a representative cider tree to invoke a bountiful crop of cider apples in the orchard. It only survives traditionally in one place, at Carhampton in Somerset (there are also commercial up-tempo revivals in the West Country), but there are references to it in South-East England in eighteenth-century Kent and up to the early twentieth century in Surrey and Sussex. The usual date for the custom was between Christmas Eve and Twelfth Night, but in the West Country this moved back about eleven days in the mid-eighteenth century to 'Old Twelfth Night' owing to a controversy over the change in the calendar in 1752. It seems likely from the evidence that in Sussex, Surrey and Kent the custom remained within the twelve days of Christmas.

The word 'wassail' is Anglo-Saxon and means 'be whole' (ie be healthy). The tradition of wassailing (which was supplanted by carol singing) consisted of a procession of wassailers carrying a wassail bowl from door to door at the Midwinter period and singing songs which asked for food, drink and money and wished good luck to the householders. Many of the tunes of these essentially pagan songs were re-used as Christian carols.

Other fruit trees as well as apple trees could be wassailed, as indicated by Robert Herrick in his poem *Hesperides*:

> 'Wassail the trees that they may bear
> You many a plum and many a pear,
> For more or less fruits will they bring,
> As you do give them wassailing.'

In the West Country it was mainly the families of the farmers or of the orchard owners and workers who wassailed the apple trees. In Surrey, Sussex and Kent, however, the custom was for groups of men and boys to travel round the orchards to 'worsle' (Sussex dialect for wassail) the trees for the usual social and economic benefits of money, food, drink, excitement and comitatus. Many god-fearing countrymen continued to believe in the superstitious importance of the custom as with other practices of essentially pagan origin which existed side by side with Christianity in rural areas.

As with other surviving rituals, social and economic factors played a large part in their survival up until the First World War and the earliest reference we have traced (apart from Herrick's poem) to apple wassailing mentions money — the rector of Horsted Keynes in Sussex, Giles Moore, recorded in his diary for 26th December 1670: 'Gave to the howling boys 6d'.

The Duncton Howlers c1897.   (Photo from the Petworth Society Magazine)

Edward Hasted in his late eighteenth-century *History of Kent* wrote:
'There is an odd custom found in these parts about Keston and Wickham...a number of young men meet together for the purpose, and with a most hideous noise run into the orchards, and encircling each tree pronounce these words:

> 'Stand fast root, bear well top;
> Give us a youling sop,
> Every twig, apple big,
> Every bough, apple enough.'

For which incantation the confused rabble expect a gratuity in money, or drink, which is no less welcome: but if they are disappointed in both, they with great solemnity anathematise the owners and trees with altogether as significant a curse.'

The words of the 'Blean Hoodening Song', sung round the parish of Blean on Christmas Eve seems to suggest a tradition of apple wassailing in East Kent as well:

> 'Three jolly hoodening boys
> Lately come from town,
> Apples or for money
> We search the country round;
> Hats full, caps full,
> Half bushel baskets full —
> What you please to give us
> Happy we shall be.
> God bless every poor man
> Who's got an apple tree.'

Hazlitt's nineteenth century *Faiths and Folk-lore* calls the custom apple howling or 'youling' and particularly refers to Devon and Sussex; he comments:
'It seems highly probable that this custom has arisen from the ancient one of perambulation among the heathens, when they made prayers to the gods for the use and blessing of the fruits coming up, with thanksgiving for those of the previous year; ...this ceremony is called Youling, and the word is often used in their invocations.'

An account from Camberley in Surrey in 1907 recalls how a group of boys came to a garden on Christmas Eve and repeated a verse similar to that quoted from Mrs Latham below. They began in a low mumbling tone, gradually rising in pitch until they were shouting and they then sounded a blast on a large cow-horn. They then went round to every fruit tree in the garden, substituting the name of that fruit in the chant.

Mrs Latham wrote in her *Some West Sussex Superstitions Lingering in 1868* (Fittleworth area):
'It is the custom in the cider districts of Sussex to "worsle" the apple-trees on New Year's Eve, and for several succeeding days, and it is considered unlucky to omit doing so. Farmers give a few pence to the worslers, who form a circle round the trees and sing at the top of their voices:

> 'Stand fast root
> Bear well top,
> Pray God send us
> A good howling crop.
> Every twig
> Apples big
> Every bough,
> Apples enow,
> Hats full, caps full,
> Full quarter sacks full.
> Holla, boys, holla! Huzza!'

and then all shout in chorus, with the exception of one boy who blows a loud blast on a cow's horn. Last New Year's Eve the mother of a sick boy told me that her poor child was sadly put out because he was not able to "worsle" his grandfather's apple-trees; and it is quite certain that both mother and child expected a total failure of the apple-crop in the grandfather's orchard to follow the omission.'

The most famous and longstanding apple-howlers in West Sussex were the Knight family of Duncton who went out on Twelfth Night and continued the custom into the 1920s. The only known photograph of traditional apple howling in the south-east was loaned by the late Captain Richard George Knight to the Chichester District Museum for an exhibition on 'Christmas Customs' in December 1982.

This photograph was taken about 1897 and shows Captain Knight's grandparents, Mrs Knight and Richard 'Spratty' Knight, 'Captain of the last band of Sussex wassailers' and Captain Knight's father Arthur William Knight, 'vice-captain of the wassailers'. Richard 'Spratty' Knight is wearing a brightly patterned costume with a string of apples around his neck and a large decorated straw hat with apples round it. He is blowing a copper and brass hunting horn, which was also lent for the exhibition and which was inscribed 'Thomas Bridger, Duncton Beagles, November 1860'. The whereabouts of the horn since Captain Knight's death is unknown. In the photograph Mrs Knight is holding a jug of cider and a cake. 'Spratty' Knight was miller at Duncton Mill and it is thought that the photograph might have been taken there.

Captain Knight remembered watching the wassailers as a small boy and recalled the noise made by the horn and others made from cows' horns. The rhyme was chanted rather than sung. He also told the 'West Sussex Gazette' the story of his grandfather's death:

> 'Spratty was evidently quite a character. He was the miller at Duncton, and he had one peculiar habit — he never came home to his tea. Instead, when he finished work, he used to drop in at the Cricketers' Inn and stay there till closing time. One New Year's Day he told his wife he was going to turn over a new leaf — he would come home to tea. "Your tea will be ready for you," she said, "as it always has been." But that evening they brought him home dead: he had fallen over in his cart and died.'

Wassailing the Apple Trees at the Kent Museum of Rural Life, New Year's Day 1992. (Photo: Simon Evans)

The Sussex folklorist Lilian Candlin obtained further invaluable information about the custom from 'Spratty' Knight's daughter, which she recounted in an article for the *West Sussex Gazette* in 1966. The howlers used to meet at 'The Cricketers' to plan their programme and would start with Mill Farm. 'Spratty' would ask the farmer if he wanted his trees wassailed.

'The gang, followed by numerous small children, then went to the orchard and 'Spratty' blew through a cow's horn which made a terrible sound. This was to frighten away any evil spirits that might be lurking around. Next one of the trees, generally the finest one, was hit with sticks and sprinkled with ale (?cider). This was a gift to the gods who looked after fruit trees.

'This completed the process of wassailing, and everyone trooped out of the orchard and went up to the farmhouse door, where they were greeted by the farmer's wife with drink and goodies. Sometimes money was given instead of good cheer.

'... The next house visited was Lavington House, and then on around the village, visiting every house that had an orchard, until they arrived at the "Cricketers" Inn, which was their last place of call.'

A letter from Mr E.F. Turner of Westhampnett was published in the *West Sussex Gazette* on 5th January 1967. Mr Turner was 'the youngest of the family living at Mill Farm, Duncton' during the last years of the wassailing there:

'The first Captain of the Wassailers I remember was Dick Knight, who had a dark spade beard. We children would become very excited as "Old Christmas Eve" (January 5th) got nearer, and on the night we used to be continually opening the back door to listen for the wassailers.

'At last we would hear them, faintly at first and gradually getting louder. It sounded as though they split into two parties, one coming down the lane on one side of the millpond and the second through the orchard on the other.

'What we heard was something like this:

'ALL TOGETHER: "Here stands a good old apple tree" (or "Nanny tree" or "Green Pippen tree", etc).

'FIRST PARTY: "Stand fast root."

'SECOND PARTY: "Bear well top."

'FIRST PARTY: "Every little bough."

'SECOND PARTY: "Bear apples now." (? enow)

'FIRST PARTY: "Every little twig."

'SECOND PARTY: "Bear apples big."

'FIRST PARTY: "Hat fulls."

'SECOND PARTY: "Capfulls."

'FIRST PARTY: "Three score sackfulls."

'CAPTAIN: "Holler, boys, holler."

'Then there would be a burst of horn-blowing, shouting and a general racket. Sometimes a big bad word would float across when someone trod in a hole or tripped over a root.

'When they reached the house, they would come into the big kitchen, with its pump, sink, bread-oven, three coppers and fireplace to sing songs and drink cider. One would be carrying the enormous cowhorn, and the Captain would have on a robe made of something like flowered cretonne and a straw hat with big apples all round the wide brim, and a bow of wide ribbon.

'His song was about "Three bold fishermen rolling down the tide" and someone with "three golden chains hanging dangling three times round." The tune was marvellous. (The song is given after this chapter.) ...I think his son sang "Two Little Girls in Blue".

'Fred Lock from Upwaltham was a regular. He sang "Bid Adieu to Old England". You might get anything from John Rowe or Bernard Connor. People said they could remember enough songs to last for two hours or so. We generally had "The Farmer's Boy", "If I Were a Blackbird", "Seagull" and "Farmer Giles" among others.

'My sisters used to stand near the doorway leading out of the kitchen, ready to go to the cellar for more cider or else to vanish for the time being if a song seemed to be getting salty.

'When they left, we used to go outside to hear more wassailing, the voices getting fainter and fainter as they went through another part of the orchard on their way to the next stopping place.

'In the course of time Dick Knight's place as Captain was taken by his son... Arthur. I think the wassailers stopped coming in the early twenties, but in 1920 or thereabouts I heard Jack Court sing "The Sunshine of Your Smile" and someone else, who seemed put out because he did not know any old songs, sang "Back Home in Tennessee".

The *Sussex Daily News* for January 8th 1919 shows the custom struggling for survival with Arthur Knight having moved out of the village:

' The war has done its best to kill our customs and habits, but customs die hard. And so one finds that the quaint ceremony of "wassailing" or charming the apple trees observed at the Down village of Duncton is one which has so far survived. Nevertheless things are not as they used to be. In years gone by when the old chief, Mr Dick Knight, was alive "wassailing" night was always a great event in the village. When the old chief died his son, Mr Arthur Knight, promised he would carry on the tradition of the village, and he has faithfully fulfilled his promise. Every year he re-visits his native village on old Christmas Eve to head the wassailers in their pilgrimage to the orchards. This year his followers numbered only three. The smallness of the band was not surprising for, as the chief remarked, "There is no one about now" — many "wassailers" are engaged in sterner work than the charming of apple trees. Despite the small number of "wassailers" and the downpour of rain, the usual visits were made to Mrs Court's, Lavington Park, Mr Seldon's, Mrs Knight, at the home of the old chief, and the mill 'neath the apples trees.'

There have been a number of revivals of apple wassailing in recent years, several involving the Chanctonbury Morris Men (eg at Henfield and Tenterden). In the absence of the ritual groups of howlers, morris men or mummers seem a fair substitute, and the Tonbridge Mummers can regularly be seen wassailing the apple trees at the Kent Museum of Rural Life at Cobtree on New Year's Day aided by Alan Austen and his shot-gun. The tradition of firing guns was a part of the west-country practice, to add to the noise which was said either to be to frighten away evil spirits or to awake the trees from their midwinter lethargy. An 1852 account from *Notes and Queries* mentions the beating of trees with sticks in Chailey, Sussex, probably for the same purpose:

'...in the neighbourhood of Chailey...a troop of boys visit the different orchards...and shout in chorus, one of the boys accompanying them on the cow's horn; during the ceremony they rap the trees with their sticks.'

Wassailing the bees also used to take place in Sussex, but not much is known about this, although it is referred to in a couple of surviving songs. The *Sussex Wassail Song*, collected by John Broadwood, has the following line: 'We'll wassail bees and apple trees until your heart's desire'. And the Vicar of Amberley, the Rev. G. Clarkson, collected the words of a song thought to have been sung to the bees on Twelfth Night from an old man in his parish:

'Bees, oh bees of paradise, does the work of Jesus Christ.
Does the work which no man can,
God made bees and bees made honey.
God made man and man made money.
God made great men to plough and to sow.
God made little boys to tend the rooks and crows.
God made women to brew and to bake.
And God made little girls to eat up all the cake.
Then blow the horn!'

The Bold Fisherman

This is a very well known folksong in Sussex and it is impossible to know which version Richard Knight sang to accompany the Apple Howling custom at Duncton. We have chosen a version collected by Clive Carey from Leonard Glaysher in the village of Borden in East Hampshire, in 1911, which is contemporary with Richard Knight's wassailing.

THE BOLD FISHERMAN.

As I walked out one May morning,
Down by the river side,
And there I beheld a bold fisherman
Come rowing down the tide.
Come rowing down the tide,
And there I beheld a bold fisherman
Come rowing down the tide.

'Good morning to you, bold fisherman,
How came you a-fishing here?'
'I've come a-fishing for your sweet sake,
All down this river clear.'

He rowed his boat up to the shore
And unto him this lady went,
And in taking hold of her lily-white hand
Which was his full intent.

Then he pulled off his fishing gown
And laid it on the ground,
And there she beheld three chains of gold
Came wrinkling three times round.

Then on her bended knees she fell,
And as for mercy called,
'I call-ed you a bold fisherman,
But I think you are some lord."

'Rise up, rise up, my dear' cried he
'From off those bended knees.
There's not one word you've said or done
That has least offended me.'

'Then come unto my father's house
And married we will be,
And you shall have a bold fisherman
To row you on the sea.'

THE MUMMERS PLAY IN SUSSEX, KENT & SURREY

The Mummers Play may have originated as a form of mime ritual involving a symbolic combat, death and resurrection appropriate to the Midwinter period when the life force is quiescent and we celebrate the death of the old year and the birth of the new. At some point the ritual acquired dramatic words and characters, and Christian respectability with the introduction of St George as hero. The plays survived mainly through the oral tradition, and references to nearly two thousand have been collect in Britain together with hundreds of surviving texts.

The development of the Mummers Play can be divided into four stages:
(i)   ritualistic origin;
(ii) christianisation;
(iii) survival into the nineteenth century for social and economic reasons;
(iv) the twentieth century interest in the plays and their revival in many areas.

(i) **Ritualistic Origin**

The concepts of death and resurrection are at the basis of most religious beliefs and in the Northern Hemisphere the midwinter solstice is an obvious time for rituals connected with such beliefs. Primitive religions contain elements of sympathetic magic in which rituals act out something which needs to happen for the well-being of the community. In most ancient cultures, drama originated through religious rituals. The death and resurrection which is at the heart of the mumming ritual is very likely a piece of sympathetic magic in origin which aims to ensure the destruction of winter and the return of the strength of the sun and fertility in man and nature by the birth of a new year and the return of the season of growth. What is not clear is whether this would originally have been achieved by a combat, or whether the symbolic death would have been passive — ie a ritualistic acting out of the death of nature in the Winter and its rebirth.

It seems likely that this ritual drama was brought into Britain by the Anglo-Saxons, since it is rarely found in Celtic areas and not at all in the Celtic languages. The word 'mumming' may derive from the Germanic verb 'mufflen' (to muffle up or disguise), and the alternative term of 'guising' has similar connotations. Medieval and sixteenth century references to mumming indicate a form of mime — eg 'As farre as I see they be mummers, for nought they say'

The West Malling Champions c1986 — leader Alan Austen third from right.
(Photo: Simon Evans)

Jaqui Bortoft as 'King George' in the Tonbridge Mummers' performance of the Bearsted Play of the Seven Champions at Allington Castle, 1985.
(Photo: Archie Turnbull)

Henri Bortoft as 'Little Slasher' in the Tonbridge Mummers' performance of the Bearsted Play of the Seven Champions at Allington Castle, 1985.
(Photo: Archie Turnbull)

Simon Evans as 'The Italian Doctor' revives both the dead combatant and 'Championing' in the Darent Valley; Darent Valley Champions at Brasted, Christmas 1989.
(Photo: Geoff Doel)

(Damon and Pithias 1571). Drawings show uniformity of costumes (some plays collected in Dorset, Hampshire and Wiltshire in the nineteenth century have similar rather than character type costumes) and often the use of leaves and greenery, perhaps linking up with that ubiquitous yet mysterious medieval figure, the Green Man. Costumes described in the nineteenth century and early twentieth centuries in many areas were of coloured ribbons sewn onto smock frocks and a student from Germany on one of our courses recently pointed out the similarity of costume in some German folk rituals, which gives the effects of uniformity and anonymity.

(ii) **Christianisation**
The entry of St George into the Mummers Play is a key factor. The Catholic Church christianised facets of paganism by using appropriate saints to sanitise heathen practices. The emergence of St George as the patron saint of England is inexplicable unless he took over from something very important in English paganism. His presence in other folk customs connected with death and resurrection (eg the Padstow Obby Oss) suggests that it his type of death and resurrection saint that is significant. The earliest surviving story about St George tells how he was martyred many times, being revived each time by St Michael. He was the most appropriate saint to take over the death and resurrection role in the Mummers Play.

Following this line of argument, it should be St George who dies and is resurrected and so it is in some northern plays. However, in the south east it is his adversary, the Turkish Knight, who dies and is revived. The reason for this is that christianisation changed the whole emphasis of the plays. They became stories of goodies against baddies, and St George, both as patron saint and representative of Christianity, had to triumph over paganism. As St George fights a crusading opponent, the Turkish Knight, it could have been at any point during or after the crusades that St George entered the Mummers Play.

The texts of the Mummers Plays have that mixture of rhyme and prose and the boastful assertions of speech found in Elizabethan and Jacobean drama and we feel the texts largely originate from this time, though there are references to mumming and some small textual links in Tudor Interludes. In the Selmeston Play from East Sussex, the Turkish Knight boasts:

> *'Here come I, a Turkish Knight,*
> *In Turkish land I learned to fight;*
> *I'll fight St George with courage bold,*
> *And if his blood's hot will make it cold.'*

The texts are clearly influenced by popular stories of St George in circulation and in particular by Richard Johnson's prose work the *Famous Historie of the Seavern Champions of Christendom* (1596) and a blank verse stage play adapted from it by John Kirke in 1638. Both these works interacted with a succession of popular chapbooks on the life of St George. After the closure of the theatres in 1642, Kirke's play entered the puppet show repertoires and chunks of his text survive in slightly debased form in many Mumming Plays.

Tony Deane as 'Old Christmas' and the Cowden Mummers (with Dragon) in a revival of the Hindhead Mummers Play, Christmas 1990.   (Photo: Geoff Doel)

The closest passages to Kirke in surviving Mummers' texts are in rhyme, as opposed to his blank verse. The St George speeches in the Mummers Plays often refer to events which are part of the St George legend in Kirke, but have no connection with the action of the Mummers Plays. For example in the West Malling play St George says:

'In comes I, St George, that noble champion bold,
With my broad axe and sword I won a crown of gold.
I fought the fiery dragon, and drove him to the slaughter,
And by these means I won the King of Egypt's daughter.'

The wording is close to the St or King George speeches in many of the south-eastern texts and those from other parts of the country.

Although St George does fight other champions in Kirke and the chapbooks, the revival scene of Mummers Plays by the mysterious Doctor, a well-travelled and learned man, is not in their versions, and it is likely that the revival was the centrepiece of the original ritual and that the Doctor was the priest/witchdoctor figure who would take the credit for the success of the sympathetic magic. The cry for the Doctor even today sounds very profound. The Guard in the Bearsted Plays summons him in these words:

'Is there a noble doctor to be found
To raise this dead man from the ground?'

The Doctor's script, however, has a clear fairground derivation, with much of the language of fairground quacks and travelling mountebanks such as described in Ben Johnson's *Volpone* and more recently by Thomas Hardy in the character of Physician Vilbert in *Jude the Obscure*. Here are the words of the Doctor in the West Wittering Play (south of Chichester), which are a mixture of rhyme and prose:

> 'I can cure the hipsy, pipsey, palsey and the gout,
> A strain within and a strain without,...
> If I break his neck I will set it again;
> I won't charge you one single farthing for my pain...

'Behold, ladies and gentlemen, see I'm not like the mountebank doctors that run about from town to town and tell as many lies in one half-hour as you find true in me in seven years! Behold, ladies and gentlemen, see, I have a little box by my side which is called "Jupiter Pills", and a little bottle in my waistcoat which is called "Golden Philosopher". Drops I one drop on his nose and another on his temple, which will strike a light in his whole body."

(iii) Survival into the Nineteenth Century

The four successive Georges on the throne in the eighteenth and early nineteenth centuries and the loss of popular interest in saints resulted in many Mummers Plays replacing 'Saint' George with 'King' George. The Chithurst Play from West Sussex has a King George the Fourth who 'won Queen Alice's fairest daughter' (instead of the usual King of Egypt's daughter). In Marshfield (Avon) the hero became King William (William IV succeeded George IV). Queen Victoria would presumably not have been amused to have been put in a Mummers Play, but the Rottingdean Play in East Sussex did change its hero to the Prince of Wales.

It seems clear from the interviews by antiquarians and folklorists in the nineteenth and twentieth centuries that the plays survived for social and economic reasons. The relative stability of many rural communities in the southeast up until the later nineteenth century meant that many traditions were handed down literally from father to son in the villages and carried out as a kind of trust. Youngsters were often involved and there was a certain status and excitement in the social interaction. The early nineteenth century was a particularly difficult time for farm labourers (the traditions being pre-industrial survived mainly in relatively stable communities in villages) and the economic benefits of money, food and drink became increasingly important, which is reflected in the begging speeches in some of the 'walk-on' characters at the end of the play. Belzeebub collected money in his dripping pan with menaces from his club:

> 'In comes I Beelzebub,
> On my shoulder I carries a club,
> In my hand a dripping pan,
> Don't you call me a jolly man?'
> (West Malling, Kent)

– from Bearsted Play, Tonbridge Mummers, 1985. (Photo Archie Turnbull)

Three Beelzebubs

– from West Malling Play, West Malling Champions, 1984. (Photo: Geoff Doel)

– from Hindhead Play, Cowden Mummers at Nellie's Folk Club, 'The Cardinals Error', Tonbridge, 1991. (Photo: Geoff Doel)

Jack Sweep in the Bearsted Play (Kent) has the lines:

> 'In comes I Jack Sweep
> All the men I have to keep
> Whether they're little or whether they're tall
> It takes a lot of money to keep them all.
> It's money I want and money I crave,
> If you don't give me money I'll sweep you all to your grave.'

Johnnie Jack, who unusually introduces the almost identical Chithurst and Iping Plays from West Sussex (his position in these plays has almost certainly been moved forward because of dramatic additions at the end) says:

> 'In comes I little Johnnie Jack,
> With my family up my back.
> Though my family be but small,
> I can scarce find bread and cheese for them all.
> Christmas comes but once a year,
> And when it comes it brings good cheer.
> Roast beef, plum pudding, mince pie,
> Who likes these any better than I?
> Christmas fare makes us dance and sing,
> Money in the purse is a capital thing.
> Ladies and gentlemen, give what you please,
> Old Father Christmas will welcomly receive.'

In the Horsell Play (Surrey) the Johnny Jack says:

> 'In comes I little Johnny Jack,
> With my wife and family up my back.
> My family large and I am small,
> I can't get enough to maintain them all,
> So ladies and gentlemen sat at your ease,
> And put in the tamberine what you please.'

In the West Malling Play (Kent), the Jimmy Jack is followed by the unusual character of the Chimney Sweep who says:

> 'In comes I, the chimney sweep,
> All the money I gets I keep.
> All the bread and cheese that I receive,
> I roll it up my jacket-sleeve,
> Ladies and Gentlemen, give me what you please.'

Old Father Christmas is the usual figure who introduces the play in the south-east, although the West Malling Play (Kent) has a 'Presenter' and in some East Midlands and North Eastern plays the ancient figure of the Fool is used. Old Father Christmas was a typical compère figure in Christmas festivities and in masques where he was sometimes called Captain Christmas. His introductory lines in the Cocking Play (south of Midhurst in West Sussex) and the Horsell Play in Surrey are typical:

The Chimney Sweep from the West Malling Play, West Malling Champions, 1984. (Photo: Geoff Doel)

Geoff Doel as Old Father Christmas in the Bearsted Play, Tonbridge Mummers, 1985. (Photo: Archie Turnbull)

> 'In comes I Old Father Christmas,
> Welcome or welcome not.
> I hope Old Father Christmas will never be forgot.'

In some of the texts, such as Bearsted (Kent), Father Christmas has a function in clearing a space for the Mummers:

> 'Stir up the fire and give us a light
> For in this room there will be a fight
> And whether we stand or whether we fall
> We'll do our best to please you all.
> Room, room, room I require...'

This links up with Thomas Hardy's description of Dorset Mummers in *The Return of the Native*:

> 'Hump-backed Father Christmas then made a complete entry, swinging his huge club, and in a general way clearing the stage for the actors proper.'

(iv) Twentieth Century Interest in the Plays and their Revivals

By the end of the nineteenth century Mummers Plays were getting scarcer. Social mobility, improved wages, loss of interest in village life and traditions all took their toll. The First World War proved the death of most of the surviving

The Tonbridge Mini Mummers performing the Kirmington Plough-Jags Play at Allington Castle, 1989 (Director Glenn Miller as musician far right). (Photo: Archie Turnbull)

plays, although there seem to have been a few in the South-East which carried on into the 1930s — West Malling, possibly Bearsted and Snodland in Kent, Thames Ditton in Surrey and Aldingbourne in Sussex. The agricultural workers and villagers' loss of interest in these plays, as in the case of folksong and morris dancing, coincided with increasing academic interest and middle class revivals. R.J. Sharp began the revival in Sussex with the formation of the Boxgrove Tipteerers in 1927, using a conflation of the Iping and East Preston Plays. After the Second World War, the great revival in morris dancing and later the second folk song revival of the 1960s, both fostered Mumming revivals.

In West Sussex the Mummers were known as Tipteerers, defined in the Rev. Parish's 1875 *Dictionary of the Sussex Dialect* as 'Mummers who go round performing a sort of short play at Christmas time.' Records of dozens of teams from small villages around the Chichester area are known — such as West Wittering, Compton, Lodsworth, Rogate, Iping, Chithurst, Cocking, Bosham, Aldingbourne, West Marden, East Marden, Graffham, Lavant, Heyshott, West Itchenor, Lodsworth and West Stoke. Three towns in this area, Petworth, Midhurst and Littlehampton are known to have had sides and the extract below seems to refer to a Chichester-based side.

A remarkable recent find sent to us by the Chichester Museum provides our earliest reference for West Sussex as well as dramatically confirming Thomas Hardy's description in *The Return of the Native* further west in Dorset of groups of quite young boys travelling some distances through the dark at night to put

The Compton Tipteerers photographed by Arthur Beckett c1911. (Doc Rowe Collection)

on their play at Christmas festivities. The extract is from the *Hampshire Telegraph* 31 December 1821:

'   MELANCHOLY CIRCUMSTANCE
Sussex 29 December

A party of youths with a view of keeping up an old custom denominated Tip Teering sallied from Chichester on Monday evening and pursued the route of Hampnett (Westhampnett), Welberton (Walberton) and Goodwood and having finished their tuneful sound they agreed in order to counteract the effects of the cold to run home, when Richard Cooper aged 13 years who was hindmost, having fallen in a ploughed field was left behind. On a search being made a short time afterward he was discovered lifeless in a field at Woodend. The extra beverage which he had taken combined with the cold and damp situation in which he fell caused his death.'

'VERDICT — *Died from the inclemency of the weather.'*

The early photograph of the Chithurst Mummers is probably typical of the costumes at the turn of the century in West Sussex, with bright ribbons and patches being sown onto farm clothes. The Chithurst costumes comprise overalls or tunics, some of chintz or cretonne, some of white calico covered with sewn on patches of fabric cut into a variety of shapes and bunches of ribbons or strips of cloth. Their hats are decorated with flowers and streamers. Only the Gallant Captain is dressed in part with a red coat and forage cap with imitation medals and badges. Their wooden swords were painted in stripes of red and blue. Father Christmas carried a painted staff topped with a bunch of holly and mistletoe and hanging ribbons. The leader carried a cow's horn to announce their approach.

In 1911, Arthur Beckett gave a description of the nearby Compton Tipteerers in his book *The Wonderful Weald*:

'There presently came into the vicarage drive a number of young men and boys fantastically arrayed; and counting them I found that there were seven, all curiously dressed but one, who had not attempted to disguise his modern clothes. But he was not the least important personage, for he carried an accordion to play upon during the march, and a cow's horn by which he announced the coming of the Tipteerers to outlying farms and houses; also his was the hat that took largesse from the spectators such time as the play was brought to its conclusion.

'Of the characters of the play I learned that these, in such sort, were named Father Christmas, St George, The Valiant Soldier, Little Johnny Jack, the Doctor and the Turk. There should have been another representing Beelzebub, but for some reason or another he did not appear, and his part was therefore taken by Father Christmas.

'...Father Christmas wore an old top hat in which was a pheasant's wing and a bunch of mistletoe; his face was blacked (and in this matter of blacking the features he followed the custom that I had previously observed in other rustics who played his part); his long beard was of horsehair. He wore a long frock-coat ... The heathen Turk wore a policeman's or soldier's helmet (the back part turned to the front) decorated with rags of many colours. Strips of coloured rags also covered his clothes; and similar decorations were worn by the other players, some having cut out pieces of tinted cloth to represent quaint animals and figures, and some wearing a high head-gear in which they had stuck pheasant's tail feathers. Wooden staves represented swords and spears...the actors themselves were the village smith and certain farm labourers, and each had his trousers braced high above the tops of his heavy soled boots.

'The Compton Tipteerers told me that the words of their play had never been written down, but that they themselves had learnt them from predecessors, and thus the play had been handed down for hundreds of years. I had some little difficulty in persuading these good fellows to commit their mummery to writing, for no single man knew the parts of his fellows.'

Despite Arthur Beckett's final comment, it is interesting to note that Old Father Christmas was able to take on the part of Beelzebub at short notice and presumably knew the lines.

The West Wittering Play has textual allusions to the Crimean War (another war involving Turks). The 'Turkey Knight' was 'Just lately come from the Russian wars to fight' and the play there often ended with 'The Dying Soldier' song from the Crimean War. More usually, though, in West Sussex, a carol ended the play, 'The Moon Shone Bright' being a favourite or 'I Saw Three Ships'. Humorous

Revival of the Chithurst Play at the Lewes Folk Club c1971.   (Photos: Geoff Doel)

corruptions crept in to some of the plays, the Turkish Knight being remembered as 'The Turkey Snipe' at Iping and Chithurst and as 'Mince Pie' at Cocking probably because of his lines:

> 'I'll cut him, and hue him as small as a fly.
> And send him to the kitchen to make a mince pie.'

Some of the lines can be quite dazzling — in Cocking St George says:

> 'I've cut this young man down, like the evening sun'

And in the West Wittering Play, the Noble Captain says:

> 'My gold shall fly like chaff before the wind
> If there is a doctor to be found.'

Moving eastwards along the Sussex coastal plain, we find references to plays at East Preston, Worthing, Ferring and Angmering. R.J. Sharp tells us that about 1890 an old man named Barnard ran a sweet shop in East Preston and took a group of boys 'tipteering' at Christmas. One of these boys was a Mr Foard who later revived the play in 1911 and Sharp joined the team as fiddler in 1912 and in 1927 merged the play with the Iping text for use by his newly founded Boxgrove Tipteerers. Barnard had originally come from Washington, where there was a play. Did he bring it with him?

A Dictionary of the Sussex Dialect phonetically quotes the opening of the Lancing Play (known from 1874-1886):

> 'In comes oi, ole' Fad'r Christmas,
> An' ham oi welc'm or ham oi naht'

An account in the Sussex Archaeological Collections for 1883 mentions Mummers at Shoreham, Southwick, Portslade, Bramber and Hove:

'St Stephens Day Sussex

Mummers still go about in Sussex on this day, and round Shoreham, Southwick and Portslade are called Tipteers or Tipteerers. Mr John Morris...saw some at Bramber in 1880 or 1881, on this day. They were dressed somewhat like clowns, and some had paper or glazed lining costumes, and they have called at houses in Portslade lately. Each one represents a different character, and carries some badge. St George and a Turk always appear. I am told that within the last 20 years a group of mummers were seen in Furze Hill, Hove.' (Sussex Archaeological Collections vol 33 1883 p256)

Accounts of two seemingly different Mumming plays in the 1890s survive from Rottingdean in East Sussex. One is described by Lucy Baldwin and Arthur Ridsdale:

'I must give a short account of the Mummers, who used to visit the different houses at Christmas time, dressed up, and acting their parts, in the dining room or kitchen, which was cleared for the performance.

'There was Father Christmas, the Prince of Wales, the Proud Turkish Knight, a Soldier, a Doctor, a Widow who wept, and Little Black Jack, who carried "his wife and family on his back"; in front he carried a tin can slung round his neck for the coppers and sixpences that he received from the onlookers. As far as I recollect the play ran thus, with more that I cannot remember:

The Rottingdean Mummers Play c1968.　　　　　　　　(Photos: Doc Rowe)

'Three knocks on the door. Enter a Mummer:
   "In comes oi, old Father Christmas: Welcome, Welcome, am I not?'
   I 'opes Father Christmas will never be forgot!
   Room, room, ladies and gentlemen, Room, room I say.
   Room for the Prince of Wiles and let 'im step this way."
'The Prince walks in with drawn sword, saying that with his sword he'd won the King of Denmark's daughter. At the same time in walks the Turkish Knight, also with drawn sword. He says: "In comes I the Turkish Knight, From my proud land I come to fight, that man of courage bold. If his blood runs hot I'll draw it cold, so let us battle try."
'Then they crossed swords, left, right, left, right, till the Turkish Knight is cut down. Kneeling on one knee he says,
   "Pardon, pardon, mighty prince, and do not cut me down,
   For I would rather lose my head than I should touch your crown."
'He is, however, cut down by the Prince of Wales, and falls to the ground. Then enters the Gallant Soldier, who walks in and says: "Ardy is my name, to be avenged of my master's death into his place I come." He fights and in his turn is defeated by the Prince of Wales. Enter next the Old Woman (usually taken by a youth), who falls weeping at the side of the prostrate figures. She is followed by the Doctor in riding costume, who is besought for help, and he replies:
   "Oh I can cure the Ipsey, Pipsey, Palsey, Gout,
   With this pill taken inside or out;
   One to his mouth and one to his heart
   Will make him rise and play his part."
"Aroise and sing," says the Prince of Wales. They all rise as Little Black Jack, with his broom, starts sweeping the floor.
   "In comes oi, Little Black Jack,
   With my family on my back.
   Money oi wants, money I craves,
   Or I'll sweep you all to your graves!"
'And then he takes round his can for the collection.
'Before they finally left, the Mummers generally gave us the whole song of "The Mistletoe Bough". This was always sung at Christmas time, as well as another with the refrain "Lying in a British Soldier's Grave" — a thoroughly gloomy wind up to a lively performance.' (Lucy Baldwin and Arthur Ridsdale: *Annals of Old Rottingdean* in *Sussex Notes and Queries* IV 1932-3.)

The famous singing family, the Coppers, were involved in this play. It ceased in 1896, but the Coppers revived it some twenty five years ago. Reginald Tiddy collected a similar play from nearby Ovingdean, which was performed about 1870 and includes a press gang officer.

The other description of a Rottingdean Play, at the end of the nineteenth century, comes from the grand-daughter of Burne-Jones the artist, who lived in North End House from 1881 to 1898:

The Chanctonbury Morris Men perform the Steyning Play at Steyning c1967.
(Photo: Geoff Doel)

The Tonbridge Mummers perform the Bearsted Play at Allington Castle, 1989.
(Photo: Fran Doel)

'It would be Boxing Night and we were all seated in the inner room waiting for the mummers. Rumours of splendid preparations for their entertainment were afoot — supper for them in the dining room with a gigantic pork pie and quantities of cider. A knock was heard at the door heralding their arrival and the audience began to wriggle on its seat with anticipation. Then noises and bumps and murmers were heard from behind the curtain and clumpings on the bare boards and at last, just before they burst with curiosity, the curtains were drawn and the play of St George and the Dragon was shown to our enchanted eyes. The actors could make but little attempt at dressing up. They were poor labourers and most of them wore smocks and leggings and with a few ribbons and pieces of coloured paper to adorn them. The smock-frock was still worn in Sussex by the older men when I was a child, and some had venerable furry top hats. The play proceeded on its usual course, St George, Turkish Knight, very unfeminine princess, Dragon and Doctor... At the end of the play they took their customary toll of the audience:

"Here come I little Devil Doubt
If you don't give me money I'll kick you out.
Money I want, money I crave,
If you don't give me money I'll kick you all into your grave!"
(The Three Houses — Angela Thirkell)

This seems to be a different play — with St George and very rare dragon and princess characters and a Devil Doubt rather than Little Black Jack at the end. Were there perhaps two groups of Mummers at the same period in Rottingdean?

Other East Sussex plays included Hastings, Crowhurst, Firle and Selmeston, but not so many are recorded on this side of the county. Inland there was a cluster of plays around Horsham.

The Chanctonbury Morris began the series of post-war revivals with Boxing Day outdoor performances including at Steyning, Worthing and Sompting and there was a vivid revival of the Chithurst Mummers Play by Vic Smith at the Lewes Arms Folk Club in the seventies. Latterly, the Merrie England Mummers have been doing stirling work, featuring the Firle Play.

Kent tends to be under-estimated and insufficiently documented by folklorists and this is especially the case with Mummers plays. Charles Kightly (who was born in Kent), for example, in his recent *The Customs and Ceremonies of Britain* writes: 'It (the Hero-Combat Mummers Play) was once performed from the Channel to the Scottish Lowlands — with the apparent exception of East Anglia, Kent and most of Wales'. Had he consulted Cawte, Helm and Peacock's *Geographical Index* of plays he would have found six referred to, but even this misses many known within the county.

Charles Kightly's statement is almost correct for East Kent, as the Hooden Horse flourished there instead of the Mummers Play, but there is an overlooked play from Dover in the Ordish collection. This text was supplied by a butler and seems to be an intriguing mixture of Kent traditional texts and 'pace eggs' texts from the North (Mumming Plays performed at Easter in the Calder Valley area in the Pennines, Rochdale etc often printed in booklets in the early nineteenth century). A number of inversions of verb and noun hint at a quasi-literary contribution or tampering.

The Kent plays are often called Plays of the Seven Champions (Parish and Shaw's *Dictionary of Kent Dialect* says that men and boys 'went a-championing') and the Dover Play features one of the original chapbook champions St Patrick (who also appears in the Symondsbury Play in Dorset). Dover also features Oliver Cromwell with his 'long copper nose' (Cromwell appears in what may be the earliest documented Mummers Play at Cork, 1685). The text of the Dover Play is given in full at the end of this chapter.

There are some early references to plays in the Darent Valley in West Kent, but most of the knowledge of these derives from some outstandingly good, but largely unpublished, field research in the 1970s by Simon Evans and Charlie Jacob, when they recorded interviews with many old men who had been in the plays before the First World War. From what we have heard from and about these tapes, they would seem to represent the most significant record of first-hand experiences of pre-First World War Mummers extant. Simon Evans has already contributed an excellent radio programme and two articles on his findings.

Simon and Charlie's researches centre on four villages along the Darent: Brasted, Riverhead, Shoreham and Sutton-at-Hone, 'each with a different version of the play and each with its own territory, performing in their own and neighbouring villages as well as in the surrounding hamlets and farmhouses'. *(The Darent Valley Champions* by Simon Evans in *A Kent Christmas* ed Geoff & Fran Doel.) The Leigh Combat Play (Leigh is near Tonbridge) was actually one of these texts taken to Leigh many years ago. Simon and Charlie organise revivals of these plays in appropriate villages (usually Brasted and Westerham) during the weekend before Christmas each year.

The Medway also had a group of plays along its settlements. Russell Thorndike knew of a Mummers Play in Rochester where he lived and this may be the one he featured in one of his Dr Syn stories (see *A Kent Christmas).* There is a reference to a play at Snodland in 1888 and Alan Austen once met an old man who told him he used to go over to Snodland to watch the Mummers earlier this century.

The Bearsted Play (near Maidstone) is referred to in Chamber's List of Texts in *The English Folk Play* as being in an 'MS of Miss Coombes'. A booklet on Bearsted School in 1939 refers to the annual appearance of the Seven Champions at the School in earlier days:

'Another event was the appearance of the Seven Champions just before Christmas. They would appear dressed in paper to suit the part and recite such strains as "I'm little Jack Sweep, all the money I get I keep" and "Here I come, Beelzebub! In my hand I carry a club, in my hand a dripping pan, don't you think I'm a jolly man." The words would be followed by the beating of the pan with the Club and we hope that the money gained covered the depreciation of the utensils.'

It is interesting that the lines given here for Jack Sweep are different from the ones in the text held by the Vaughan Williams Memorial Library quoted earlier in the chapter. They are similar to the Chimney Sweep lines at West Malling. The original ms disappeared, but another was supplied to the English Folk Dance and Song Society by Carl Willetts, who advertised in *The Kent Messenger* and was sent a play which was formerly acted at Bearsted School. The Bearsted Play is succinct and acts very well in pubs; it features Father Christmas, Guard, King George, Little Slasher, The Doctor, Jack Sweep and Beelzebub. It is a favourite of the Tonbridge Mummers and Hoodeners, a team founded in 1981, which performs a number of plays as no local Tonbridge text has yet turned up. The Tonbridge Mummers also have a lively junior team, the Mini Mummers.

A text also survives for the West Malling Mummers Play (another Medway village). This had a Presenter instead of a Father Christmas, and St George, Bold Slasher, Doctor, Beelzebub, Jimmy Jack and Chimney Sweep. Alan Austen has revived the play and it is normally performed in the pubs of West Malling on the Saturday before Christmas. Alan has met people in the area who remembered the play between the wars (one gentleman remembered it in the thirties) and there was apparently a non-speaking part of a gravedigger (opportunities for a thesis on the connections with *Hamlet* here!). In the Dover text the Doctor refers to gravediggers as being his friends (presumably as his remedies assist their vocations!).

Mr J.A. Dawson, the Hon. Sec. of The Rotary Club of Malling, wrote to Alan Austen about the play in 1982:

'... I was able to recall the Mummers at West Malling...about 1912 or 1913. My memory is of about 4 players dressed in highly coloured military uniforms which probably came from the Boer War era. They would visit houses just before Christmas and have sham sword fights outside the front doors of houses with much worthy shouting conversation of which in my youthful 8 years I could not understand a word.'

The text of the play has a footnote:

'The actors wore outlandish costume and all had blackened faces except St George, who wore a brass helmet with a plume resembling that of a Life-Guardsman.'

The face-blacking would presumably be for disguise, achieving the same effect as strips of ribbons hanging over the face in the west of England.

Although the chances of meeting anyone who has been in or seen a traditional Mummers Play in the south-east (as opposed to a revival) is now remote, there are still the secondary sources of children remembering bits of texts quoted by their fathers. Several times after giving talks on Mummers Plays, people in the audience have given us fragments of lost plays their fathers used to recite and which they often did not realise the significance of until attending the talk. For example here is a quote from a lady, whose father (a Mr Martin) lived at Gillingham (Kent) as a young man and used to recite to his family:

The Tunbridge Wells Mummers c1987 (organiser Jack Hamilton second from left).
(Photo from Jack Hamilton)

St George and the Dragon from the Hindhead Play, Cowden Mummers at Nellie's Folk Club, 'The Cardinal's Error', Tonbridge, 1991. (Photo: Geoff Doel)

> 'Here comes I old Beelzebub,
> On my head I carry my tub,
> In my hand my frying pan
> Don't you think I'm a funny old man.'

Is this from a lost Gillingham play?

Jack Hamilton founded an unusual, but very effective, Kent side in 1972 and wrote a play for them: in his own words:

'The Tunbridge Wells Mummers was formed in 1972 with a few pub friends who had never heard of mumming. The play is a composite of the most common elements of recorded plays with the addition of local notable Beau Nash, a prominent figure in the life of Tunbridge Wells in the mid-eighteenth century. For this part I composed a few lines of no consequence but gave the character a key part in the play. The performance was designed to be performed in the constricted space likely to be found in a crowded pub bar: to this end a rehearsal of the longsword fragment in the performance was rehearsed in a telephone kiosk.'

As a part of the revival in the Tunbridge Wells Play, the Turkish Knight blows a ping pong ball into the air which the Doctor has to catch.

In Surrey, Mummers were called Tipteerers in the south of the county and Mummers in the north. One of the best Surrey texts (printed at the end of this chapter) is from Hindhead and features a rare Dragon as well as Old Christmas, St George, Turkish Knight, Doctor, Beelzebub and Little Johnny Jack. This could be the play reported near Farnham in the 1860s. The Cowden Mummers give spirited performances of this play every Christmastide.

There are reported to have been plays at Croydon, Coulsdon, Barnes, East Molesley, Hascombe, Horsell, Newdigate, Frensham and Thursley in the nineteenth century, with reports of a Thames Ditton Play in 1939. Texts survive for Frensham in north Surrey and Thursley in the West and at Horsell a text was taken down from some travellers about 1908, featuring Father Christmas, King George, the Turkey Snipe, Doctor and Belsie Bob.

A.J. Mumby recounted being visited by Mummers at his house at Pyrford on Boxing Day 1883 — half a dozen in number and they sang *God Rest Ye Merry Gentlemen*. John Broadwood, earlier in the century, collected *The Sussex Wassail Song* on the Surrey–Sussex border, which was sung by a group of boys to the tune of *God Rest You Merry Gentlemen*. It is probable that the carol adopted a wassailing tune. George Sturt (the writer George Bourne) saw Mummers near Farnham in 1897.

Another revival team in Surrey is the Buckland Shag Mummers team, named after a dragon who used to sit on the side of the Shag Brook (a tributary of the Mole) between Reigate and Dorking.

It is to be hoped that the revival teams in the south-east continue to thrive and that more young people take up mumming. Schools and young people's organisations could make more use of them as they are great fun to act in and to watch. Traditionally they were men or boys only, but most revival teams include ladies as well, who often make the most ferocious combatants!

THE COMPTON TIPTEERERS PLAY

From Arthur Beckett's *The Wonderful Weald* (1911); see our previous chapter for description of the play.

Valiant Soldier
In come I, a roamer, a gallant roamer,
Give me room to rhyme,
I've come to show you British sport
Upon this Christmas time.

Stir up your fire and give us a light,
And see we merry actors fight.
For in this room there shall be shown
The heaviest battle ever known
Betwixt St George and the Turkish Knight.
If you don't mind to believe these few words I've got to say
Let the old Gentleman of all slip in and clear the way.

Father Christmas
In come I, old Father Christmas, perhaps welcome, perhaps not,
I hope old Father Christmas will never be forgot.
Although I've got but a short time to stay
I've come to show you British sport to pass the time away.
I have just lately come firing down
From the borders of the City of London town.
I've just turned one-hundred-and-seven years of age,
I can hop, skip and jump like a blackbird in his cage.
Room, room unto me, I say;
After this let St George slip in and clear the way.

St George
In come I, St George, that man of honour and courage stout and bold;
With my sword and spear all by my side I have won twelve crown of gold;
It was I who fought the Fiery Dragon and brought him to great slaughter,
And by those means I hope to win the King of Egypt's oldest daughter.

Valiant Soldier
In come I, a soldier stout and bold;
As I was walking along the road

I heard great wonders and talks of you, St George;
If I was to meet thee I would prick thee through and through,
And make thy precious blood to flow.
Come in, thou Turkish Knight,
While we are here to-night
We are not to bear the blame.

Turkish Knight

In come I, the Turkish Knight,
Just come from Turkey-land to fight.
I'll fight thee, St George — that man of honour, (of) courage stout and bold,
Let not his blood be ever so hot I will quickly make it cold.

St George (aside)

Dare say you would, too!
Stand back, stand back, you noble Turk, or by my sword you'll die,
I'll cut your giblets through and through, and make your buttons fly.

Turkish Knight

Pardon me, St George, pardon me I crave.
And ever more will I be thy Turkish slave.

St George

You saucy little rascal! Ask me to spare your life after being so confounded bold! Been up in my best room and stole my best clothes! Not only that, but took a watch from my pocket. I'll up with my sword and run thee through and through.
(Does so. Turk falls.)
(To Father Christmas) Behold, old man, and see what I have done,
I've cut your noble champion down just like the evening sun.

Father Christmas

Seems as if you have done it now.

St George

Well, Father, what was I to do? He gave me the challenge three or four times and why should I deny?

Father Christmas

Go home, you saucy rascal. Behold, yea, is there a doctor to be found?

The Doctor (coming forward)

Yes, old Gentleman, there is a doctor to be found
Who can quickly rise your poor son who lies bleeding on the ground.

Father Christmas
Do you call yourself a doctor?

The Doctor
Yes, old gentleman, I am a doctor.

Father Christmas
You comes in more like three-ha'porth o' bad luck than you do a doctor.

The Doctor
Don't matter what I come in like, or what I look like, as long as I can rise your poor son who lies bleeding on the ground.

Father Christmas
I don't know as you can do it yet. What is your pay?

The Doctor
Ten pound is my pay;
Full fifty I'll have out of you before you go away,
You not being a poor man.

Father Christmas
I can't pay so much money as that;
I'd sooner let him lay there and die.

The Doctor
Stop, old gentleman, I'll satisfy you with quarter-part o' that.

Father Christmas
That's according to what you can cure.

The Doctor
I can cure all sorts of diseases:
The itch, the stick, the palsy, the gout,
Raging pains within and without,
This young man's arm's broke, his leg's broke,
Calf swollen up as big as a tan-leather bottle.

Father Christmas
As big as a wooden-legged bottle, more like it.

The Doctor
Rec'lect, old gentleman, I an't been about all my time a-life without knowing nothing.

Father Christmas
Where did you get all your learning from?

The Doctor
I travelled for it: I travelled France, 'Merica, Spain and Dover,
I travelled the wide world all over.
I served my 'prenticeship in St John's Hospital seven year all one summer.

Father Christmas
Seven year all one winter, more like it.

The Doctor
I could rise this young man before your face. So could you if you know'd how and which way. So I did and so I can. I rose my poor old grandmother after she had been dead a hundred and ninety-nine years. She cut her throat with a ball o' rice; I slipt in and sewed it up with a rice-chain.

Father Christmas
Talk about what you run-about doctors can do!

The Doctor
Look here, old gentleman. I had a man brought to me the other day; indeed, he was not brought to me, he was wheeled to me in a left-handed wheel-barrow. He could not see anything without opening his eyes, and could not speak without moving his tongue.

Father Christmas (aside).
More would you,
Or else you would not talk so fast as you do.

The Doctor
Look about, old gentleman, another curious trick I'll show you before I go away. Look deedy, or else you won't see it kick, and troublesome cure yourself for me.
(Going).

Father Christmas
Stop, doctor, stop! Come and try one of your pills on my poor son, sooner than having him lying about here all this Christmas.

The Doctor
I've got a little bottle in my waistcoat trouser breeches pocket, what they call *okum, slokum, elegant plaint.* I don't.

Father Christmas
What do you call it?

The Doctor
That makes no difference, so long as you drop
'One drop on the young man's heart and another on his brain' —
He will rise and fight bold Champion again.
(Doctor proceeds to cure Turk.)

Turkish Knight
How long have I been lying on this floor?
Ten minutes or more,
I've been urged and scourged and dragged from door to door.
To-morrow morning at the hour of five,
I'll meet thee, St George, if I am alive.

St George
To-morrow morning, at the hour of ten,
I'll meet thee spring guard, with fifty thousand men.
I'll hage thee, gage thee, and let thee know
That I am St George over old England.
Go home, go home, you Turkish Knight,
Go home to your country and fight;
And tell those 'Mericans what I've done:
I've killed ten thousand to thy one.
Now I am off (to) my discharge.
God bless the Turk, likewise St George.

Johnny Jack
In come I, little Johnny Jack,
Wife and family at my back.
Though I am so little and small
I am the biggest rogue among you all.
If any man offend me I bring him to a stand
(Query: line omitted.)
Cutter and Slasher is my name,
From those blessed wars I came,
It was only me and seven more
Fought the battle of a score,

And boarded a man-of-war.
Cut them up as fine as any flying dust,
Sent them to cook-shop to make mince-pie crust.

St George
What little rattling, prattling tongue is that I hear?

Johnny Jack
That's mine, sir.

St George
If I hear any more of that you and me will have a cut before we part;
On my heart, before we part.

Turkish Knight
In come I, cuts and scars,
Just returning from those wars;
Many a battle I've been in,
Many a battle I have seen.
I've seen St George and all his royal men;
Cannon ball passed by my head with spite —
I lost my height;
Twice through the head I've been shot,
Which makes my brain boil like my old pot.
What more can be bolder?
Enter in the Valiant Soldier.

Valiant Soldier
In come I, a valiant Soldier, Bold and Slasher is my name;
With my sword and spear all by my side, I hope to win this game.
Now I am a soldier stout and bold,
I make many a man's blood run cold.
Now I am returning from those wars.
(To Turk) I am a man like you, full of cuts and scars.
Pull out your sword and fight, pull out your purse and pay,
Satisfaction I will have before I go away.

Turkish Knight
No satisfaction will I give thee, no more will I pay,
But this battle we will fight both manfully before we go away. *(They fight.)*

Johnny Jack
In come I, Twin-Twan,

The left hand of this press-gang;
I pressed all these bold mummers sin'
The time the ship-of-war came in.
Although my name is Saucy Jack,
Wife and family at my back;
Out of eight I've got but five,
And they are almost starved alive.
Some in the workhouse all alone,
And these at my back must be helped before I get home;
So if any man would like to fight let him come on;
I urge him, scourge him, fight him with spite;
And after that I fight the best man under the sky.

Father Christmas
You saucy little rascal! Challenge your poor old father and all the sons he's got?

Johnny Jack
Yes; I urge him, scourge him, fight him with spite,
And after that I fight the best man under the sky.

Beelzebub
In come I, old Belsey Bob,
On my shoulders I carry my nob,
In my hand a dripping pan,
Don't you think I'm a funny old man?
Christmas comes but once a year,
And likes to give you jolly good cheer;
Plum-pudding, roast beef — who likes that better than anybody else?
To-night I'd like a glass of grog; a glass of beer'll suit these chaps to-night.
Price, sir! price, sir! give you a bit of a rub,
A halfpenny towards the rent, and a penny towards the grub.
Price, sir! price, sir! and my old bell shall ring,
Put what you like in my old hat and then these chaps will sing.

Immediately the Tipteerers joined in singing the Mummers' Carol:
As we come out on a Christmas Day,
Christmas Day, Christmas Day,
As we come out on a Christmas Day
So early in the morning.

We saw three ships come sailing by,
Come sailing by, come sailing by,
We saw three ships come sailing by
On Christmas Day in the morning.

And who should be in those three ships?
Those three ships, those three ships?
And who should be in those three ships?
'Twas Joseph and his Fair Lady.

He did whistle and she did sing,
And all the bells on earth did ring,
For Christ our Saviour he was born
On Christmas Day in the morning.

Jack was nimble and Jack was quick,
Jack jumped over the candlestick;
Jack was nimble and Jack was quick
On Christmas Day in the morning.

THE DOVER MUMMERS PLAY

From the Ordish Collection; we discuss this text in the chapter on plays; printed by kind permission of the Folklore Society.

Old Father Christmas
Room, room here gallants, give us room to rhyme
We've come to show activity at this Christmas time.
The time to make mince pies doth now appear
So we are come to act our merriment in here.
We are the merry actors that traverse the street.
We are the merry actors that fight for our meat.
So blow up your fire and give us light,
For in this house there will be a fight.
And if you don't believe what I say,
Stand in St George, thou champion and clear the way.

St George
I am St George from good old England sprung.
My famous name throughout the world hath rung.
Many bloody deeds and wonders have I shown
And made false tyrants tremble on their throne.
I followed a fair lady to a giant's gate,
Confined in dungeon deep to meet her fate.
Then I resolved with true knight errantry

To burst the door and set the captive free.
Far have I roamed, oft have I fought, and little I rest;
All my delight is to defend the right and succour the opprest.
I freed fair Sabra from the stake,
What more could mortal man undertake?
I fought them all courageously,
And still have gained the victory;
And I will always fight for liberty,
And here I draw my bloody weapon.
Show me the man that dare me stand
I'll cut him down with mighty sword
And with a courageous hand.

Turkish Champion

Here come I, the Turkish Knight,
Come from the Turkey land to fight.
I'll take St George to be my foe
And make him yield before I go.
He brags to such a high degree,
He thinks there was never a knight but he.
So draw thy sword St George! thou man of courage bold,
If thy English blood is hot, soon will I fetch it cold.
I'll cut you and slash you and make mince pie of you.
I'll bake you in an oven, and send you back to Turkey-land,
And after that I'll fight every champion in Christendom.

St George

Where is the Turk that will before me stand?
I'll cut him down with my courageous hand.

Turkish Champion

Draw out thy sword and slay,
Pull out thy purse and pay,
For satisfaction I will have
Before I go away.

St George

I'll run my sword through your body
And make you run away.
(They fight. The Turk is slain.)

St George

I am the chief of all these valiant Knights.
We'll spill our hearts' blood for old England's rights.

Old England's honours we will stand maintain,
We'll fight for old England once again.
I challenge all my country's foes.

Turk's Father
Oh George, oh George. What's this you've done!
You've killed and slain my only son.
My only son, my only heir,
See how he lies stretched and bleeding there.

St George
He had me challenged to fight and how could I deny?
How low he lies, who held himself so high.

Turk's Father
A doctor, a doctor, ten pounds for a doctor,
Is there never a doctor can be found,
To cure this man of his deep and deadly wound?

Doctor
Here am I a Doctor pure and good,
And with my broad sword I'll staunch his blood,
And if this young man's life I'll save,
Full fifty guineas I must have.

Turk's Father
What can you cure Doctor?

Doctor
All complaints within and without,
From a cold in your head to a touch of the gout.
Moreover than that, if you bring me an old woman of three score and ten,
If the knuckle bone of her big toe is out of joint I can put it in again.
Nay, more than that by far I will maintain,
If you lose your head or heart, I'll give it you again.
Then here's a Doctor rare, who travels much at home,
So take my pills and cure all ills, past, present and to come.
I never met a gravedigger yet who to me objected.
If a man gets 19 bees in his bonnet I can fetch 20 out.
I've got in my pocket, crutches for lame ducks,
Spectacles for blind bumble bees, pack-saddles for grasshoppers,
And many other needful things.
Surely I can cure this poor man.

Turk's Father
What are your drugs, Doctor?

Doctor
Easy peasy pens midgels oil and humble bees gravy,
The juice of the beetle, the sap of the pan,
Three turkey eggs nine miles long.
Put all that together in a midge's bladder,
Stir up with a gray cat's feather.
Put three drops of that in Jack's left ear
And if he is a living man he will rise up and sing a song.

Turkish Champion (sings)
Once I was dead but now I'm alive,
God bless the Doctor that gave me the prize.
We'll all shake hands and fight no more,
And we'll be as good brethren as we have been before.

Oliver Cromwell
Here come I, Oliver Cromwell, as you may all suppose,
I've conquered many nations with my long copper nose.
I made the French to tremble and my enemies to quake,
And I beat my opponents until their hearts did ache.

St Patrick
Here comes I, St Patrick, in shining armour bright.
I am a famous champion and a worthy Knight.
And this truth I fain would learn ye
I banished serpents, toads and frogs
From beautiful Hibernia.
And the reptiles all ran races
As they took their way into the sea
And they have never shown their faces since.
Who was St George but St Patrick's boy?
For seven years he fed his horse on oats and hay,
And afterwards he ran away.

Saint George
I say by George you lie, Sir!
Pull out your purse and pay Sir!

Saint Patrick
Pull out your sword and try Sir!

Saint George
I'll pierce thy body full of holes,
And make your buttons fly.

(They fight, Saint Patrick runs away)

Beelzebub
Here come I, Beelzebub,
Over my shoulder I carry my club.
And in my hand, a dripping pan
And I think myself a jolly old man.

Devil Doubt
Here comes I, little Devil Doubt,
If you don't give me money I'll sweep you all out.
Money I want and money I crave,
If you don't give me money I'll sweep you all to your grave.
I have a little box, under my arm,
Eight or ten shillings will do it no harm.
All silver no brass
Bad halfpennies don't pass.
Ladies and gentlemen rise up and shake your feathers
For you needn't think that we are blethers,
For we are the boys that can give you fun
If you will give us share of your Christmas bun.

Song
God bless the master of this house
Likewise the mistress too
And all the little children
That round the table go.

With your pockets full of money
And your barrels full of beer,
We wish you all a merry Christmas
And a happy New Year.

THE HINDHEAD MUMMERS PLAY (SURREY)

This very interesting part of a Surrey Mummers text, which includes a speaking Dragon, was kindly passed to me by Tony Deane who has merged it with a Kent text to form the vivid play currently performed by the Cowden Mummers.

The text seems to have originally have been passed from a Dr A. St Johnston to Haslemere Museum on 18th January 1939 as *Fragments of the Mummers Play as played in the neighbourhood of Hindhead until the (First World) War.* Dr St Johnson lists the characters as: Father Christmas, St George, Turkey Snipe, Doctor, Doctor's Boy and Dragon, but the text shows three more combatants, without giving their names — 'Royal Russian King', 'Bold French Officer' and 'Bold and Slasher'. The combat between the Royal Russian King and the Bold French Officer seems to have Crimean War connotations and is most interesting.

As well as adding in these names, we have made two alterations in printing Dr St Johnston's text. One is to switch round the two Father Christmas speeches, so that his reference to the king walking in is followed by that event, and the other is to substitute 'rise' for 'ride' in the Doctor's resurrection speech concerning the Frenchman.

The fragment ends abruptly with the entrance of the Turkey Snipe (corruption of Turkish Knight) and anyone wishing to use the text could exclude this character (as there are plenty of fights as it is) or add in dialogue and fight between St George and Turkish Knight from another play.

Almost certainly the Hindhead Play would have had a begging character, such as a Johnny Jack or Beelzebub, at the end, and a concluding song and, again these can be 'borrowed' from other texts to complete the play.

Dr St Johnston also noted that:

'The Doctor's Boy played a tambourine, the Dragon a concertina and a fiddle was also played. Part of the costume was tall paper hats with ribbons.'

Father Christmas

Here comes I Father Christmas
Welcome or welcome not
And I hope that Father Christmas
Will never be forgot.
We shan't come here to laugh and jeer
And then we give good cheer,
With plum pudding, roast beef and mince pies
And who likes that better than I?

I roam, I roam for my brave gallants all
You give them leave to rhyme,
And they will show you the activity
On this merry Christmas time.
The activity of youth, the activity of age,
The sights that never were seen before
Upon the stage.
So if you don't believe in what I sing
Walk in the royal accession king
And clear the way

The Royal Russian King

Here am I the Royal Russian King
Born in christendom.
I fear no man but Him,
French, Dutch, Portuguese or Turk,
No man can do me any hurt,
For my head is made of iron,
My body is lined with steel
(Hang it to my knuckle bone
And fight him in the field).

Bold French Officer

A bold French officer am I
And now I come my fame to try,
Long time I've made the country fly,
And now I come to make you die.
So mind your head and guard your blows,
For now I come to face all foes.
So it's battle which you and I are going to try,
To see which here on this floor shall die.

(fights with swords, Frenchman falls)

Doctor's Boy

Oh Doctor, is there a Doctor to be found
Here, or ready near this town,
That can cure a deep and deadly wound,
And raise this champion from the ground.

Doctor

Oh yes, here's a doctor to be found,
Here and ready near this town
That can cure a deep and deadly wound.

Doctor's Boy
What, can you cure all sorts of diseases?

Doctor
Bring me an old donkey been dead twenty years,
If he will crack one of my pills,
That will rise him from the ground;
So if this is the crime you have had before,
Rise up young man and fight once more.

Bold and Slasher
In comes I the Giant bold
And Slasher is my name,
Wheresoever I go they tremble at my fame,
Wheresoever I go they tremble at my sight,
No lord nor champion shall with me fight.

(Fights — the Russian falls)

Doctor's Boy
Fifty pounds for a noble Doctor.

Doctor
Oh yes, the chance of a little money.
Now fifty pounds, did you (say) sir?

Russian
Yes, and be quick.

Doctor
Here Jack, take a little of my flippeley
Down your tippeley,
Rise up and fight again.

St George
Here I am, St George,
From Britain do I spring,
To fight that fiery dragon,
My wonders to begin,
I'll clip his wings, he shall not fly
I'll cut him down, or I'll die.